God Sent a Rainbow
and Other Bible Stories

Paintings by Malcah Zeldis

Retold by Yona Zeldis

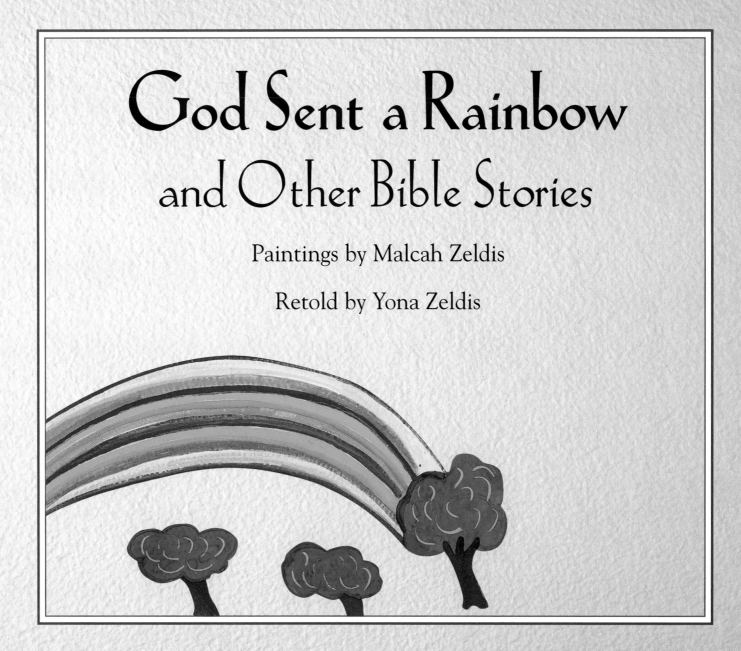

God Sent a Rainbow
and Other Bible Stories

Paintings by Malcah Zeldis

Retold by Yona Zeldis

The Jewish Publication Society
Philadelphia • Jerusalem

For Constance Marks, a sister under the skin.
—Y.Z.

For Jason Marcus and Sharon Camel.
—M.Z.

Acknowledgments—My thanks and gratitude to my wonderful editors, Bruce Black

and Ellen Frankel, for their skillful minds and wise hearts.
—Y.Z.

Text © 1997 by Yona Zeldis
Paintings © 1997 by Malcah Zeldis
Design of text and cover: Ox + Company, Inc.
Printer: Alesi Graphics, Inc.

Manufactured in the United States of America

Library of Congress Cataloging-in-Publication Data
McDonough, Yona Zeldis.
        God sent a rainbow and other Bible stories / by Yona Zeldis: illustrated by Malcah Zeldis.
            p.   cm.
        Summary: Presents a series of stories from the Old Testament, including God's creation of the world, Noah
        and the ark, the sacrifice of Isaac, Joseph and his brothers, and the giving of the Ten Commandments to Moses.
        ISBN 0-8276-0591-9 (cloth)
        1. Bible stories, English—O.T. [1. Bible stories—O.T.]   I. Zeldis, Malcah, ill.   II. Title.
        BS551.2.M384 1997
        221.9'505—dc21   96-46241
                                                                                    CIP
                                                                                    AC

Contents

The Creation of the World

BEFORE GOD CREATED HEAVEN AND EARTH, THERE WAS ONLY A HUGE, WATERY space blanketed by darkness. Then God swept over the waters and cried, "Let there be light!" Suddenly, bright, clear light was everywhere. When God saw this, God knew that it was good. God then separated the light from the darkness and God called the light "day," and the darkness, "night." This was the very first day. ★ On the second day, God created the sky, separating the heavens above from the earth below. ★ On the third day, God gathered all the waters into one place and called them "sea." The dry land left behind was called "earth." But the earth had no life, so God created trees, bushes, plants, fruits, and flowers to grow on it. Again, God looked at these creations and saw that they were good. ★

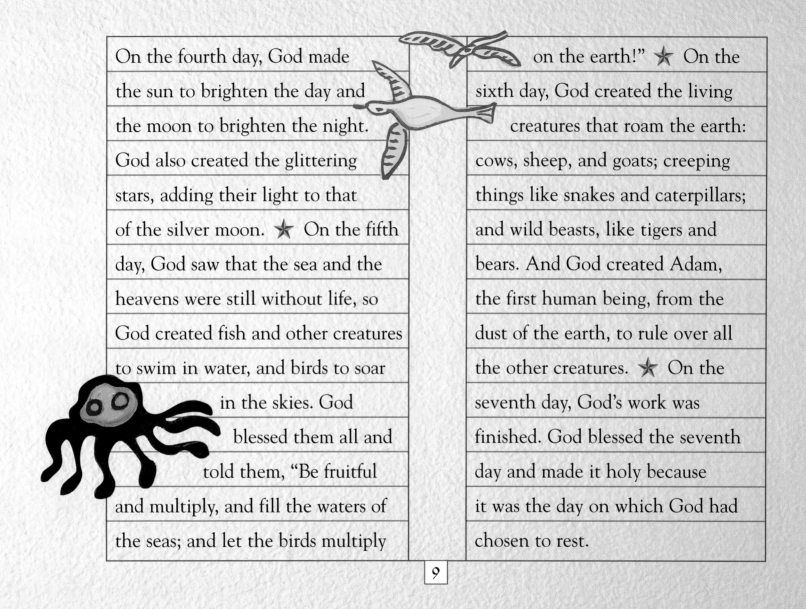

On the fourth day, God made the sun to brighten the day and the moon to brighten the night. God also created the glittering stars, adding their light to that of the silver moon. ★ On the fifth day, God saw that the sea and the heavens were still without life, so God created fish and other creatures to swim in water, and birds to soar in the skies. God blessed them all and told them, "Be fruitful and multiply, and fill the waters of the seas; and let the birds multiply on the earth!" ★ On the sixth day, God created the living creatures that roam the earth: cows, sheep, and goats; creeping things like snakes and caterpillars; and wild beasts, like tigers and bears. And God created Adam, the first human being, from the dust of the earth, to rule over all the other creatures. ★ On the seventh day, God's work was finished. God blessed the seventh day and made it holy because it was the day on which God had chosen to rest.

The Garden of Eden

GOD PLANTED A GARDEN IN THE EAST CALLED EDEN. THERE GOD PLACED Adam to care for the beautiful plants and trees that grew within it. ✦ God then brought all the birds, animals, and fish to Adam and listened as Adam named them one by one. But since Adam was made in God's image, none of these creatures was fit to be his companion and mate. God said, "It is not good for the man to be alone; I will make a fitting helper for him." So God cast Adam into a deep sleep, and, while he slept, took one of Adam's ribs, closing up the place where it had been taken. From this rib God created a woman whom Adam named Eve, the mother of all life. When Adam looked at her, his heart rejoiced for he knew that she could be his friend and mate, and that he would never be lonely again.

God Sent a Rainbow

ADAM AND EVE HAD CHILDREN, AND SOON THE EARTH was filled with people. But they were evil, and this made God sad. God said, "I will blot out from the earth the people whom I created—together with beasts, creeping things, and birds of the sky; for I regret that I made them." ★ There was one man, however, named Noah, whose good deeds pleased God, and so God told Noah to make an ark out of wood and Noah obeyed. Into the ark marched Noah, his wife, his three sons and their wives, and a pair of each kind of animal—a male and a female. ★ Then the sky opened

and it poured for forty days and forty nights. The waters swelled and rose. As the ark drifted on the waves, Noah, his family, and all the animals remained safe inside. ★ When the waters began to go down, Noah opened the window of the ark and sent out a raven, which flew back and forth until the waters went down part way. Then he sent out a dove to see if the ground was now dry. The dove could find no resting place for her feet, so she returned to the ark. ★ A week later he sent the dove out again. In the evening, she came back clasping a freshly plucked olive leaf tightly in her beak! Then Noah knew that the waters had gone down. Still, he waited seven more days. When he sent the dove out for the third time, she did not return. ★ God told Noah, "Come out of the ark!" So Noah and his family, and all the

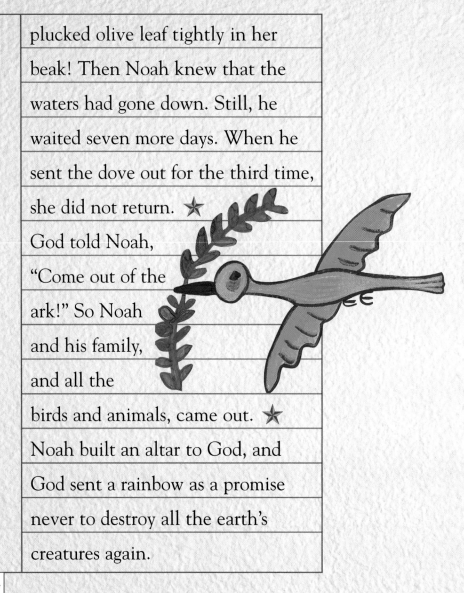

birds and animals, came out. ★ Noah built an altar to God, and God sent a rainbow as a promise never to destroy all the earth's creatures again.

The Tower of Babel

 **A**FTER THE FLOOD MEN AND WOMEN TRAVELLED FROM the east and found a valley in the land of Shinar. There they began to build an enormous tower because they wanted to be like God. All the people on the earth at this time spoke a single language and used all the same words, so the work sped along quickly and the tower—made from bricks—soon grew to a dizzying height. ★ God looked down and saw the tower. It made God angry, but God remembered the promise never to destroy the world again. Instead, God said,

"Let us make a babble of human language, so that they no longer understand each other when they speak." And so the place was called "Babel." 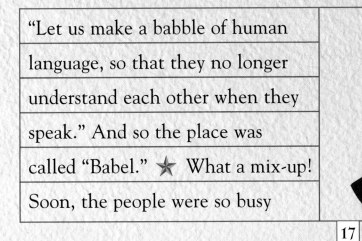 What a mix-up! Soon, the people were so busy fighting and shouting that they forgot their work on the tower. From that time on the people of the world were divided into different nations and spoke different languages.

17

Abraham Is Chosen

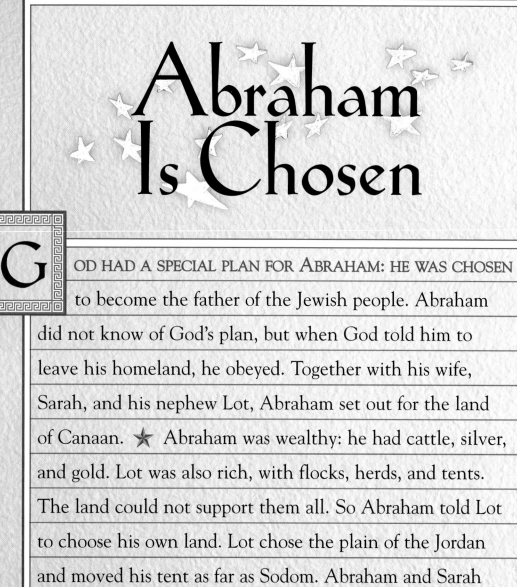

GOD HAD A SPECIAL PLAN FOR ABRAHAM: HE WAS CHOSEN to become the father of the Jewish people. Abraham did not know of God's plan, but when God told him to leave his homeland, he obeyed. Together with his wife, Sarah, and his nephew Lot, Abraham set out for the land of Canaan. ★ Abraham was wealthy: he had cattle, silver, and gold. Lot was also rich, with flocks, herds, and tents. The land could not support them all. So Abraham told Lot to choose his own land. Lot chose the plain of the Jordan and moved his tent as far as Sodom. Abraham and Sarah

settled in Canaan. ★ One day God came to Abraham in a vision and said, "Do not be afraid, Abraham. I am your shield. Your reward shall be great." ★ Abraham said, "But what can you give me since Sarah and I have no children?" God led Abraham outside his tent and said, "Look up and count the stars if you can. You shall have as many descendants as there are stars in the skies." Abraham looked up and saw the stars sparkling in the dark night. And he believed in his heart that God's promise would one day come true.

The Sacrifice of Isaac

GOD KEPT THE PROMISE MADE TO ABRAHAM. ALTHOUGH Abraham and Sarah were now old, Sarah gave birth to a son, Isaac. Abraham and Sarah loved their son very much, and he loved them. ★ When Isaac had grown into a man, God told Abraham to take his beloved son to the land of Moriah and sacrifice him as a burnt offering. When they reached the place, Abraham told the two servants to wait with the donkey while he and Isaac went to worship. Isaac carried the wood for the offering. Abraham carried the fire and the knife. ★ Isaac said,

21

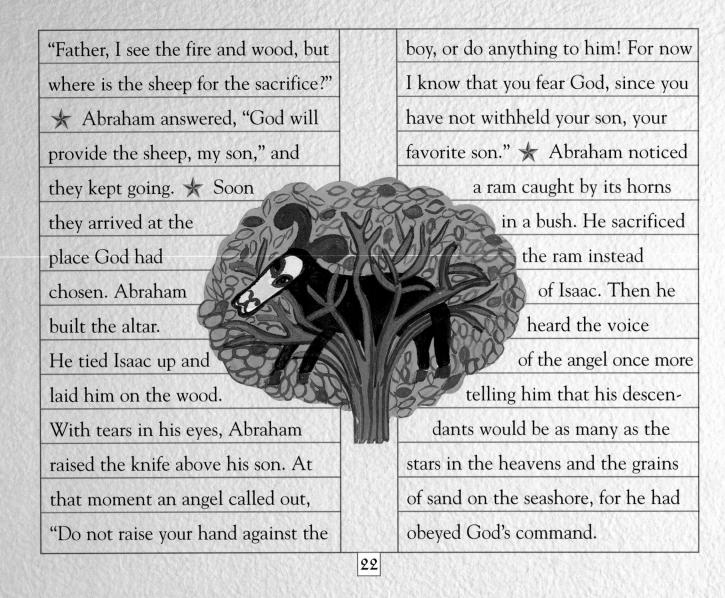

"Father, I see the fire and wood, but where is the sheep for the sacrifice?" ★ Abraham answered, "God will provide the sheep, my son," and they kept going. ★ Soon they arrived at the place God had chosen. Abraham built the altar. He tied Isaac up and laid him on the wood. With tears in his eyes, Abraham raised the knife above his son. At that moment an angel called out, "Do not raise your hand against the boy, or do anything to him! For now I know that you fear God, since you have not withheld your son, your favorite son." ★ Abraham noticed a ram caught by its horns in a bush. He sacrificed the ram instead of Isaac. Then he heard the voice of the angel once more telling him that his descendants would be as many as the stars in the heavens and the grains of sand on the seashore, for he had obeyed God's command.

Jacob's Ladder

I SAAC MARRIED REBEKAH, WHO BORE HIM TWIN SONS. ESAU WAS BORN FIRST. His skin was red and covered with hair. Jacob followed right behind, his tiny hand grasping his brother's heel. As they grew, so did their differences: Esau liked the open fields and was a skillful hunter, while Jacob was a quiet boy who stayed near the tents. Isaac loved Esau best, but Rebekah loved Jacob. ★ With his mother's help, Jacob tricked his older brother Esau out of his birthright and Isaac's blessing. When Esau discovered his brother's trick he was furious and vowed to kill him. Rebekah told Jacob to go live with her brother Laban in Haran until Esau's anger cooled. ★ Jacob set out for Haran. When the day ended, he lay down alongside the road, using a stone for a pillow. As he slept, he dreamed: ★

A ladder stretched from the earth all the way to heaven. On it God's angels went up and down. Then God spoke to him, "I am the God of your grandfather, Abraham, and the God of Isaac. The land on which you are lying I will give to you and to your children. Your descendants shall be as many as the dust of the earth. You shall spread all over, east and west, north and south. I am with you, and will guard you wherever you go, and I will bring you back to this land." When Jacob awoke, he was amazed. "Surely God is in this place, and I did not know it!" He set up his stone pillow as a sacred altar before continuing on his way.

Jacob Wrestles with the Angel

JACOB LIVED IN HARAN FOR MANY YEARS. FIRST HE married Leah, Laban's oldest daughter, and then he married Rachel, her younger sister. Soon Jacob was a father, and owned many servants, camels, donkeys, and flocks of sheep and goats. ★ After Jacob had worked for Laban for twenty years, God told Jacob that it was time to return home. Jacob gathered his wives, his twelve children, and all their possessions and set out for Canaan. ★ On the way he worried about meeting his brother Esau. Would Esau still be angry with him for the trick he had

played so many years ago? Would he wish to harm Jacob's family? Jacob sent his men ahead with many presents for his brother, hoping these gifts would convince Esau to treat him kindly. Then he sent his children, his wives, and their servants to safety across the river Jabbok. ★ Jacob was left alone. Suddenly, a stranger appeared. Jacob did not know that the stranger was really one of God's angels. The two began wrestling. They struggled all night long. Even though the angel pulled Jacob's hip joint out of place, he still could not beat Jacob. ★

Finally the angel said, "Let me go, for it is morning." ★ "I will not let you go unless you bless me," Jacob replied. ★ "What is your name?" asked the stranger. ★ "Jacob." ★ "Your name will be Jacob no longer," said the angel, "but instead you will be called 'Israel,' because you have struggled with God and with human beings and you have won." ★ Just as the sun's golden light filled the sky, the angel blessed Jacob and vanished.

Joseph the Dreamer

JACOB, NOW CALLED ISRAEL, HAD TWELVE SONS AND

a daughter. Of all these, he loved Joseph best and had

a special coat of many colors made for him. Joseph's brothers

grew jealous when they saw it. ★ One night Joseph had

a dream. "We were binding sheaves of wheat in the field," he

told his brothers in the morning. "My sheaf stood up straight,

while all of yours came and bowed down to it!" ★ "Does

this mean that you will rule over us?" asked his brothers.

And they hated him more than ever. ★ Then Joseph had

another dream. "The sun and moon and eleven stars bowed

down to me!" he told his brothers and father. And his brothers' hatred continued to grow. ★ One day, Israel sent Joseph to see how his brothers were doing with the flock. ★ When his brothers saw him in the distance, they said, "Here comes the dreamer! Let's kill him and throw him into a pit!" ★ But Reuben, the oldest brother, convinced the others to throw Joseph into the pit still alive. They tore off his coat of many colors and left him without food or water. When a group of Ishmaelites came by, another brother, Judah, persuaded the others to sell Joseph to them as a slave. So Joseph was sold for twenty pieces of silver. ★ His brothers dipped his coat of many colors into the blood of a goat they had slaughtered. When they brought the bloody coat to their father, Israel recognized it instantly: "Joseph's coat! Some wild animal has killed and eaten him!" And Israel wept bitterly over the death of his favorite son.

Joseph and His Brothers Reunited

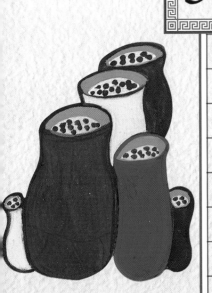

J OSEPH WAS SOLD INTO SLAVERY IN EGYPT, BUT BECAUSE OF HIS GIFT FOR understanding dreams he rose to power until only Pharaoh stood above him. When a famine struck all the countries in the region, only Egypt, under Joseph's wise leadership, had food. ★ Jacob sent ten of his sons to Egypt to buy food for their family. But he kept back Benjamin, the youngest, for he feared something bad might happen to him. ★ When the brothers came before Joseph, they did not recognize the young boy they had thrown into the pit years before, but Joseph knew who they were. To test his brothers, Joseph accused them of being spies and imprisoned them for three days. Then he made them leave one brother in prison while the others went back to get Benjamin. ★ At first Israel refused to

let Benjamin go with them. But when all their grain was gone, he gave in. So the brothers travelled back to Egypt. When Joseph saw Benjamin, he went into another room to hide his tears. 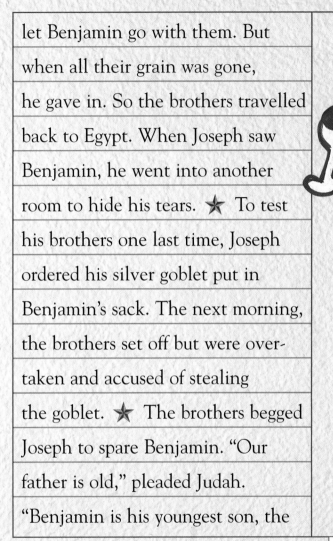 ★ To test his brothers one last time, Joseph ordered his silver goblet put in Benjamin's sack. The next morning, the brothers set off but were overtaken and accused of stealing the goblet. ★ The brothers begged Joseph to spare Benjamin. "Our father is old," pleaded Judah. "Benjamin is his youngest son, the only remaining son of his mother, Rachel. If you take this boy from him, our father will die too. Let me remain in his place." ★ After sending away his Egyptian servants, Joseph broke down and wept. ★ "I am Joseph," he declared. "Do not be ashamed or angry that you sold me into slavery, for God sent me here to save you for a great deliverance. Bring my father here, and you shall all be near me; I will take care of you now." ★ And then, amid tears of joy, Joseph and his brothers embraced.

Pharaoh's Daughter Saves Moses

A FTER MANY YEARS, JOSEPH AND HIS WHOLE FAMILY DIED, AND A NEW PHARAOH arose to power in Egypt, one who did not know Joseph. This pharaoh made the Israelites slaves, forcing them to make bricks for his temples and tombs. Their lives were filled with hard work and cruelty. But still they survived and flourished. ★ Terrified that the Israelites would soon out-number them, Pharaoh decreed that all newborn Israelite boys were to be drowned in the Nile River. When the Hebrew midwives Shifra and Puah disobeyed him, Pharaoh ordered the Egyptians to kill the Israelite babies themselves. ★ One Hebrew woman, Yokheved, hid her beautiful baby boy for three months, and then placed

him in a little basket among the reeds in the river and told her daughter, Miriam, to watch what happened to the baby. ★ Miriam saw Pharaoh's daughter and her servants walking to the river to bathe. The basket caught the princess's eye and she told her slave girl to get it. Inside the basket she found a baby crying. "This must be one of the Hebrew children," she said and she drew him out of the water. ★ "I will call him Moses—the one drawn out—for I drew him out of the water," announced the princess, who adopted him as her son. ★ And Moses grew up in Pharaoh's palace.

38

Moses Sees the Burning Bush

ALTHOUGH MOSES WAS RAISED AS A PRINCE IN PHARAOH'S court, he knew he was an Israelite. One day he saw an Egyptian master beating a Hebrew slave. Looking to make sure no one saw him, he killed the Egyptian, then hid his body in the sand. When Pharaoh learned of the Egyptian's death, he ordered Moses killed, too, but Moses escaped to the land of Midian. There Moses met the seven daughters of Jethro, Midian's priest, when they came to water their father's flock. A group of shepherds tried to chase them away but Moses drove the shepherds away, then helped the

women water their flock. When the women told their father what had happened, he was pleased and gave Moses his daughter, Zipporah, as a wife. ★ One day Moses was in the desert tending Jethro's flock. He came to the sacred mount of Horeb, the mountain of God, and noticed a bush on fire. Miraculously, its branches were not scorched by the flames. ★ God called to Moses from the bush. "Do not come closer. Remove your

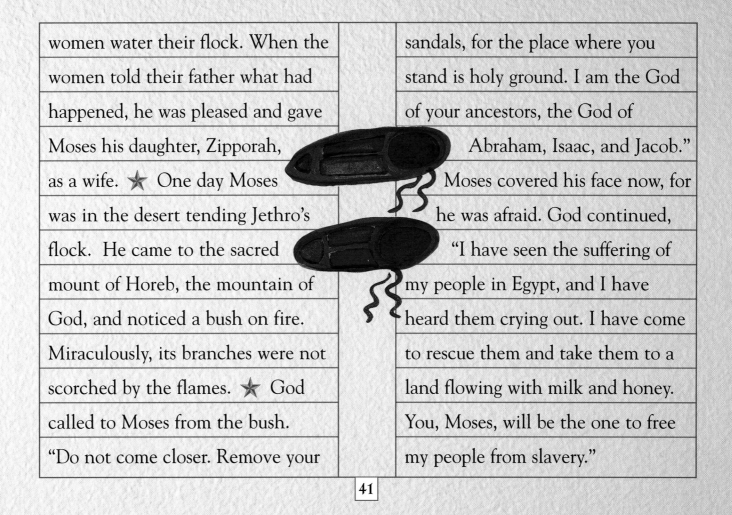

sandals, for the place where you stand is holy ground. I am the God of your ancestors, the God of Abraham, Isaac, and Jacob." Moses covered his face now, for he was afraid. God continued, "I have seen the suffering of my people in Egypt, and I have heard them crying out. I have come to rescue them and take them to a land flowing with milk and honey. You, Moses, will be the one to free my people from slavery."

God Swept the Sea with a Strong Wind

 OSES RETURNED TO EGYPT WITH HIS OLDER BROTHER, AARON. THEY TOLD the Israelites of God's promise of freedom, and went to Pharaoh to plead for their people's release. Moses tried again and again, but still Pharaoh said no. ★ Angry, God brought down ten terrible plagues upon the Egyptians. After each plague Pharaoh promised to set the Israelites free. But as soon as the plague was over he broke his promise. Then one night God struck down the first-born of every Egyptian while sparing the first-born of the Israelites. Only then did Pharaoh cry out, "Go! Leave my people and my land!" ★ Fearing Pharaoh would change his mind again, the Israelites left in such a hurry that their bread dough— prepared for the journey—had no time to rise, and they took it just as it was. ★

Pharaoh did change his mind. He gathered an army of six hundred chariots, horsemen, and foot soldiers, and chased the Israelites to the shores of the Sea of Reeds. ★ Then God spoke to Moses. "Raise your staff over the sea!" Moses obeyed, and all night God swept the sea with a strong wind until the sea bed was dry and the Israelites could pass through safely. The Egyptians followed right behind, but the waters came rushing back over the chariots and the army, drowning them all. ★ When the Israelites saw the Egyptians lying dead on the shore, they truly understood the power of God, and God's servant, Moses. Moses and Miriam each sang a song to God, and Miriam led the women in a joyful dance of freedom.

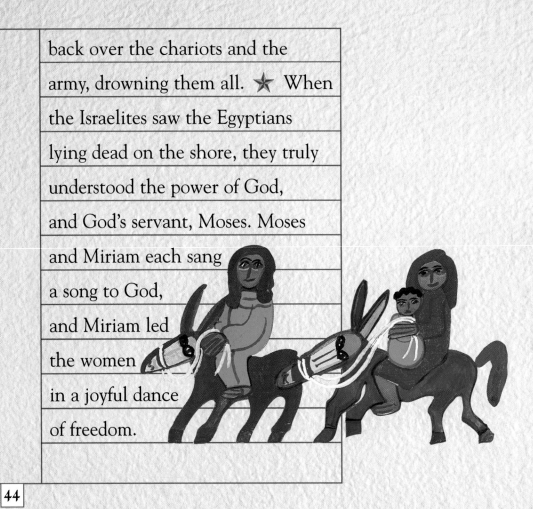

Moses Receives the Law

 AFTER WANDERING IN THE DESERT FOR TWO MONTHS, the Israelites finally reached Mount Sinai. Moses climbed up the mountain and spoke with God, who promised to treasure the Israelites and to make of them a holy nation if they obeyed God's laws. Moses told the elders of the tribes what God had said. "We will do what God commands," they answered. ★ God told Moses to tell the people to prepare themselves, for God would come down the mountain and speak directly to them. So they bathed and put on fresh clothes. On the third day, Moses gathered the people

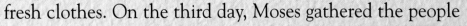

together at the foot of the mountain. ★ A thick cloud rolled down over the mountain. The Israelites saw lightning, smoke, and fire. They heard great claps of thunder and the mighty sound of a ram's horn. The earth trembled, and they trembled too. Then they heard the voice of God: ★ *I am God, who brought you out of Egypt.* ★ *You shall have no other gods but me, nor shall you worship idols.* ★ *You shall not take God's name in vain.* ★ *Remember the Sabbath day and keep it holy.* ★ *Honor your father and your mother.* ★ *You shall not murder.* ★ *You shall not commit adultery.* ★ *You shall not steal.* ★ *You shall not be a false witness against your neighbor.* ★ *You shall not be jealous of your neighbor's wife or of your neighbor's house, ox, donkey, or anything else belonging to your neighbor.* ★ These were the Ten Commandments that God gave to Moses and the people of Israel.

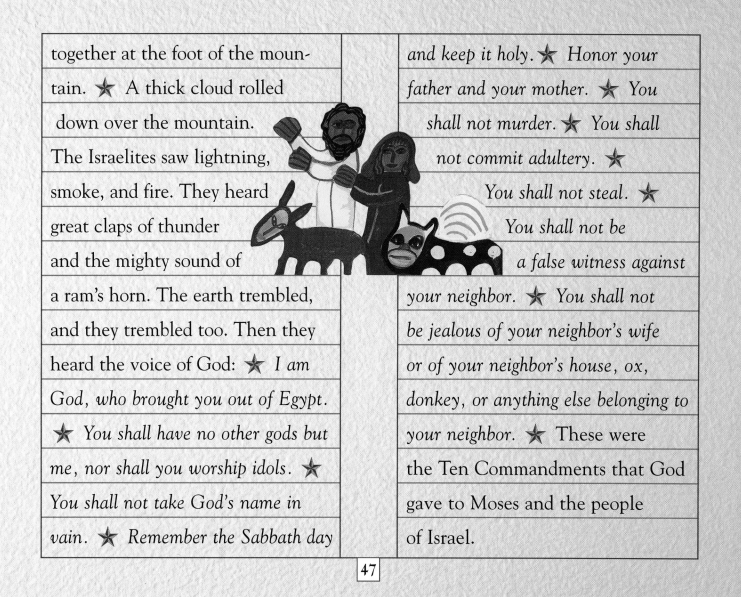